HILLS OF F AND IRON

'Heads of the Valleys Heritage'

by PETER MORGAN JONES

*'The scene at night is beyond conception.
The immense fires give a livid hue to the faces of the workmen
and cause them to present a ghastly appearance while the
sounds of steam rolling mills and mass hammers worked
by machines or wielded by brawny arms preclude
any possibility of being heard when speaking'.*

Old Bakehouse  Publications

First published in June 1992

ISBN O 9512181 9 0

Published by
Old Bakehouse Publications, Church Street,
Abertillery, Gwent NP3 1EA
Telephone: 0495 212600   Fax: 0495 216222

Made and printed in U.K.
by J.R. Davies (Printers) Limited

2

FOR BARBARA, MARTYN AND JANE

This work would not have been possible without the great assistance and encouragement provided by Welsh Industrial & Maritime Museum, Cardiff: Special thanks are due to Dr. Bill Jones, Gordon Hayward and others of that institution whose contribution has been outstanding.

Tredegar Town Council has also been very supportive, demonstrating a belief that, while facing a totally different future, valley communities should not ignore their industrial heritage. My sincere thanks go to all concerned.

Any errors and omissions are mine alone, ascribable to an intention of presenting a broad view rather than historical minutiae.

Peter M. Jones, March 1992.

FOREWORD

Nearly a decade ago the Welsh Industrial and Maritime Museum, (National Museum of Wales) organised an exhibition on the area Peter Jones writes about in this book. It is an area with a fascinating history for it was here, along the north-eastern rim of the coalfield, that South Wales experienced the impact of industrialisation for the first time. Here, too, the first industrial communities developed, towns like Blaenafon, Ebbw Vale, Tredegar, Rhymney, Merthyr and Aberdare. Entitled simply 'The Heads of the Valleys', (I wish we had thought of the evocative title 'Hills of Fire and Iron'!), the exhibition tried to show that, although these towns undoubtedly have their own distinctive identities, nevertheless they all underwent a common historical experience. The exhibition proved to be a very popular one and it was displayed for lengthy periods at various venues in the area

In preparing the exhibition we were fortunate to have the help of many local historians and photographic collectors whose involvement greatly improved the final product. Thanks to their co-operation we were able to collect, and subsequently preserve, an important archive of historic illustrative material and a significant part was featured in the display. Among the enthusiasts was the author of this book, at the time Head of Art at Tredegar Comprehensive School. Peter was kind enough to allow us to draw freely from his formidable knowledge of the history of the locality - no reader of this book can be in any doubt about either the existence of extent of that knowledge - but also to prepare a complementary exhibition on the local history work which pupils at the school were carrying out under his supervision.

Many of the illustrations in this book are, in fact, from the Welsh Industrial and Maritime Museum's archive. During the course of his research the author has been a frequent visitor and has also helped us acquire new material he has unearthed during the course of his research or, in some cases, has taken himself. At the museum we regard the collection and preservation of images as one of the most crucial elements in our work of recording the history of industrial and maritime activity in Wales, and of the communities that grew up because of that activity. Historic photographs etc. can be an invaluable source of information on, and insight into, the past, especially as today the pace of change is increasing rapidly. From the standpoint of the end of the Twentieth Century, photographs of, say, steelmaking in Ebbw Vale in the 1950's, or a carnival in Tredegar in the 1970's, are as 'historic' or 'old' as ones taken at the start of this century. The Heads of the Valleys area is only one of the many parts of Wales which are now unrecognisable compared to what they were even a generation ago.

I am delighted to have been asked to write a Foreword for this book because of the opportunity it offers to thank the author in print for his help and interest in the work of the Welsh Industrial and Maritime Museum over the years. It is also a great pleasure to have been able to contribute to such a welcome publication. Because of this well-written and absorbing account, I am sure that many - local people and visitors alike - will gain a greater appreciation of the immensity of the historical experience of those who once lived in the 'Hills of Fire and Iron' and realise that, at this very time, they are witnessing another irrevocable transformation.

Dr. Bill Jones, Assistant Keeper, Welsh Industrial and Maritime Museum.

An early Nineteenth Century balloonist would have seen it best of all. As his craft drifted over Hirwaun, moving eastwards before the prevailing winds towards Blaenavon, the land beneath would have seemed a dark, smoke-soiled ribbon, patterned with flame and glare. To the South industry was beginning to extend deeply into green valleys, its waste heaps obliterating what had once been farms. Northwards, empty moorlands stretched away to the Usk Valley scarp, the new industrial settlements ending abruptly where the coal and iron seams ceased. An interlace of horse-drawn tramways marked where furnaces were supplied with raw materials from open-cast 'patches' and 'levels', and their output taken to canal or sea-port. Here, along this mile-wide 'outcrop' the land seethed and fumed as men, women and children, toiled in what had become the iron-making centre of the world.

To a lowland dweller watching furnace-glare sullenly lighting night skies, the whole upland area was 'Merthyr' a wild, lawless region where any fugitive from justice could seek and obtain refuge. Agricultural workers, scraping a living from subsistence-level farms came to regard the purple and red-lit clouds as the beckoning of a greater prosperity.

For more than a hundred years furnaces roared across the Monmouth and Glamorgan hills but by the century's end their fires were dying one by one: Even though some were to blaze once more during the 1914-18 War, with its ending they went out for ever. At Ebbw Vale, in 1938, there was a miraculous re-birth when the Richard Thomas Steelworks was constructed. Now even those furnaces have vanished and little remains of an amazing and incredible era. Industrial empires and ruling dynasties have vanished: Flowers, trees and grass hide the pit-waste and furnace-slag that was their legacy.

AGRICULTURAL DAYS

In the latter years of the Nineteenth Century, Archdeacon Coxe made his celebrated tour of Monmouthshire during which he was to visit the Ebbw Valley and, incidentally, traverse its future Garden Festival - Wales site. Even though some industry existed in the area, it was small-scale and agriculture still predominated:

'As we proceeded the vale expanded and numerous farmhouses with small enclosures of corn and pasture occupied the slopes of the eminences and spread down into the narrow plain on each side of the river. The whitened walls and brown stone of the detached buildings gave an air of neatness and gaiety to the surrounding landscape.'

The Archdeacon, gazing at these scenes, was also intriged by the prevalence of red flannel shirts.

'By means of Mr. Williams, (who spoke Welsh), I enquired why the man wore a red shirt and why he preferred flannel to linen? He replied that 'it was warm and comfortable, prevented colds and could be worn longer without washing'.

Coxe then arrived at Blaenau Gwent, the upper valley where there were *'two furnaces, several forges, steam engines and much rebuilding of machinery for smelting and forging. They belong to Hill, Harford and Co.'* He described, also, the ironmaster's residence, its site later becoming part of the Festival.

'The residence of Mr. Harford is attended with considerable advantage and adjacent grounds have been cleared and cultivated together with an extensive tract of moor which formerly only produced heather and fern (now) converted to pasture. It yields excellent hay.'

There were other vivid descriptions of this upland region shortly before iron-making was to tear it apart.

'In visiting the farm houses in the hilly districts I was struck with the enormous quantities of bacon with which they are stored, frequently observing several ranges of flitches suspended from the ceilings of the kitchens. Bacon is almost the only meat served at the tables of the farms and, with vegetables and with the production of the dairy, forms their diet. Thin oat cakes are a common substitute for bread and the repasts are enlivened by the cwrw, their national liquor. It is a new ale in a turbid state before being clarified by fermentation. The beverage is extremely forbidding to the sight and nauseous to the taste. Principal articles of diet for labourers are potatoes, oatcakes, milk and cheese together with an inferior species of cwrw. The small cottages are all provided with a garden and some are enabled to keep a cow which ranges the commons for subsistence. The comforts are increased by the abundance of fuel, whether coal or wood, which abounds in every part of the country …the condition of the peasantry in Monmouthshire is very advantageous.'

This idyllic picture of a happy, self-sufficient, people was not always borne out by other travellers. However, Cox was impressed by what he saw:

'It is impossible', he continued, *'to travel in Monmouthshire without being struck by the appearance of cheerfulness and neatness which results from the custom of whitewashing their houses on account of the*

abundance of lime. This operation is annually performed within and without, which greatly contributes to the health of the inhabitants. The whiteness of these buildings on the sides and summits of hills surrounded by foliage of different hues considerably heightens the picturesque effect of the diversified landscapes.'

Archdeacon Coxe was witnessing the very end of a culture that had continued, largely unchanged, for hundreds of years; indeed, certain elements may have originated during the Bronze Age. Rough tracks and poor communications led to isolation and in-breeding; even itinerant pack-men might be reluctant to venture into an area where trade was as much by barter as coin. However rosy was the Archdeacon's view, the reality was a subsistence-level economy and a life hard, backward, and brutish. The coming of industry would change it all.

THE UPPER VALLEYS

The valleys into which Archdeacon Coxe ventured, ran south from high northern moors, their pattern dictated by a far more ancient river system. Formerly the whole region had been covered by another landscape complete with its own particular drainage. When this ancient surface was eroded away these rivers retained their established courses, although now cutting down into differently-tilted rock strata. This 'superimposed-drainage' makes the region geologically unusual in that its rivers flow against the rock-grain.

Ridges between the valleys are capped by a hard 'Pennant' series which resists erosion: Unable to easily-widen their beds, rivers have cut downwards into underlying carboniferous series: Settlements established lower down the valleys to exploit deeper coal seams may lose some hours of sunlight. At the head of the Sirhowy and Ebbw Valleys these harder Pennant rocks are absent enabling far wider valley floors to be formed.

PREHISTORIC TIMES

The Archdeacon was witnessing a remote community whose ancestors had probably long-occupied the same lands. In the valleys themselves farming and later industrial exploitation would have obliterated any prehistoric evidence; alternatively it is possible that early human settlement along valley floors was inhibited by swamp and dense tree-cover. Certainly, the region is capable of producing massive trees; any protected from grazing stock attain considerable height and girth and indicate what the valleys once contained. Oak and Silver Birch are indigenous, but most other species that are introduced grow well. Human development has always affected tree-cover; systematic clearance for fire and shelter probably took place from very early times.

Discoveries on the valley ridges and adjacent northern moorlands indicate that there was once extensive human occupation and activity. Bronze Age burial cairns and cists are relatively com-

9

monplace, several being visible against skylines. Discoveries of Bronze Age hoards have been made; one of these, at Princetown (SO 110 098), near Tredegar, was of spearheads deposited in an offertory well. These religious offerings were of a quality indicative of a relatively prosperous economy.

Throughout the upland area many flint artifacts from as early as Mesolithic times (c. 10,000 yrs.) have been found. Other Neolithic (c. 5000 yrs.) and Bronze Age (c. 4000 yrs.) flints suggest a continuing occupation. Much evidence exists for cultivation at surprising heights above sea-level; apart from many hut sites and enclosures there are also extensive stone/earth banks which may have been tribal boundaries. Local moorlands, once covered by open woodland, were stripped for hut-building and fires: Continual grazing, especially by sheep, has prevented natural regeneration; this animal above all others is the enemy of upland recovery. For thousands of years local moors were occupied, hunted and farmed, only becoming totally depopulated with the arrival of industry.

Examples of Prehistoric sites:

Many upland sites are only accessible to experienced walkers; the area is featureless and therefore dangerous during poor visibility. However, several sites are readily accessible, particularly along the northern scarp where limestone provided a drier occupation surface and sweeter grass. Two such areas are:

1. East of the Beaufort - Llangynidr road at SO 161 173, is the Blaen Onneu cairn field and settlement area. Here are c. 40 field-clearance stone mounds, clear evidence of cultivation; some may also have been used for burial purposes. Several hut-sites and enclosures, perhaps of Bronze Age date, have been found along the adjacent 'Cwalca' scarp.

2. Near the above, at SO 163 173, is 'Carreg Waun Llech', a prehistoric standing stone sited centrally in a large open area. Hut-sites and enclosures on the neighbouring scarp may be associated.

FROM ROMAN TO NORMAN PERIODS

Little evidence exists for any Roman presence in this area, although a centurial burial stone near New Tredegar in the Rhymney Valley, together with some unprovenanced coins, may indicate 1st Century campaigns against local Silures.

The only 'Roman' road is that recorded by Archdeacon Coxe, a claim later supported by Theophilus Jones in his 'History of Brecknockshire'. This was said to be a paved way running north along the ridge between Sirhowy and Rhymney Valleys. Particularly clear near Bedwellty Church, it continued N. eventually traversing 'Trefil Ddu' ridge W. of Trefil (around SO 120 128). A matching route in this latter area is marked on the 1832 Ordnance Survey Map but no positive traces now remain. This may have been an ancient route: Many such tracks would have been used by Romans whose roads were not always ruler-straight and well-engineered.

It seems probable that bloody, albeit small-scale, conflicts took place locally throughout the Roman period, especially during the Leg. 11 Augusta's campaigns against local tribes.

THE DARK AGES

Evidence for post-Roman occupation is equally scanty although, near the present Trefil Quarries, (SO 073 132) stands the Cwm Criban inscribed stone, one of several such memorials sited in Breconshire. Inscribed with Irish 'Ogham' characters, a system whereby letters are represented by groupings of horizontal lines, these provide evidence that people of Irish origin had entered the region in the post-Roman period and were burying their dead near well-used tracks. Extensive enclosures at nearby 'Buarth-yr-caerau', i.e. 'Fields of the forts', may be contemporary.

SAXONS AND NORMANS

It is highly-likely that tribesman of 'Gwynllwyg', of which Blaenau Gwent was a part, participated in the constant lowland-raiding during this period. Indeed, such attacks may have originated as far back as the Bronze Age.

During the Seventh Century expansion of Offa's Anglo-Saxon kingdom of West Mercia the Welsh frontier was pushed back to the Monnow River. It is noteworthy that Offa's Dyke was not built across the Herefordshire Plain, almost certainly because the Saxon penetration had not then ended, nor the frontier stabilised. This movement seems to have been one more of assimilation than displacement: Lowland Welsh life went on very much as before, there being little truth in the commonly-accepted belief that 'the Welsh were driven onto the hills'. Upland tribes were there by choice, following a largely pastoral tradition; lowland-Welsh were predominantly arable farmers whose relative prosperity stimulated raiding by their poorer neighbours. Along the Southern March were the long-established hatreds and feuds that would hinder Welsh unity.

The hill-man was a pastoralist warrior, counting his wealth 'on the hoof', regarding those who tilled the soil as little better than serfs. A hill-man's prosperity, even survival, was weakened by the Welsh tradition of 'Gavelkind' whereby, upon death, any property was divided equally between children. Ever-decreasing holdings of land or stock prompted attacks upon neighbours, even family, in order to survive. Such raids, and their ensuing blood-feuds, became the norm; Welsh tribes would often co-operate with invaders against neighbours, or invite their assistance in such attacks. Glamorgan fell to a handful of Norman adventurers in such a way and, near the Rhymney River, a Norman/Welsh force defeated a Welsh army at the battle of Mynydd Carn.

In the same way constantly-raided lowland Welsh came to appreciate the arrival of war-like newcomers able to provide greater protection. Even so, Domesday Book of 1086 was to declare much of their land as 'wasted'. Upland regions such as Blaenau Gwent would have been subjected to retaliatory raids; according to contemporary sources the lowland-Welsh were always 'first in any attack on the hills and the last to leave'. This whole region was, perhaps for millennia, a country of internecine feud and bloody conflict.

The frontier zone was to change following the Norman Conquest. This warrior society had a grain-based economy and farmed up to c. the 600 foot (185m) contour. Upland Welsh found themselves isolated by chains of castles controlling strategic river crossings or trackways. No castle could, of its own accord, 'control' an area, only oversee movement through it at a particular point: The majority of early castles around the hills were sited more to prevent raiders returning with live-stock rather than in any hope of keeping them out. Even though Norman overlordship was claimed over the uplands - Blaenau Gwent becoming part of the Lordship of Abergavenny - this was largely nominal with the edge of cultivation dividing two fundamentally-opposed and hostile cultures. Raiding continued, as did retaliation; higher 'Welshries' following their traditional ways; lowland Welsh, willing to adopt new ideas, being more likely to prosper. Slowly the uplands did change but real peace did not come to the Marches until Henry VII's accession in 1485. Even so, in spite of Saxon, Norman and English, Hereford city was considered Welsh in character as late as the Eighteenth Century.

MEDIEVAL AND POST-MEDIEVAL PERIODS

Even though raiding ceased allowing upland peoples to benefit from peaceful contact with the lowlands, their life remained basic and traditional. Transhumance, the custom of moving flocks to higher pastures in summer, continued. Welsh society was based upon scattered 'tref' or homesteads rather than centralised settlements. For example, in Archdeacon Coxe's day there were at least thirty small farms in the upper Ebbw Valley, largely dependent upon cereals and the pig.

Fairs, a means of barter and trade, had been a feature of local life for centuries although this must have been hindered by poor communications. Travel was, predominantly, along the ancient, possibly prehistoric, ridge-ways, their significance indicated by associated churches. Suddenly, all this was to end when a way of life, basically unchanged since prehistoric times, would be swept away.

THE REASON WHY?

Mineral deposits outcropped along the coalfield's entire northern edge but were at their richest, and most suitable for iron-making, between Hirwaun and Blaenavon. Nature had provided enormous quantities of iron-stone or 'mine' together with fire-clay used to line early furnaces. Well-wooded valleys were a source of charcoal for primitive smelters but even when later furnaces required coke there was coking-coal in abundance. Carboniferous Limestone necessary as a furnace-flux outcropped a little distance north and the Millstone Grit with which it was capped provided silicas for their refractory bricks and linings. Everything necessary for the production of iron in vast quantities lay just to hand.

The modern A 465(T) 'Heads of the Valleys', road running between Brynmawr and Hirwaun, approximates to the coal-basin edge. Generally South of its line is that narrow strip of land where carboniferous rocks, rich in coal, iron-stone and fire-clay, rise to the surface. Even today, after intensive exploitation, these minerals are still present in quantity when the overburden is removed. Modern open-cast operations exploit what remains: Former 'pillar and stall' mining methods left large blocks of coal untouched to provide roof-support.

The limestone basin containing these rich deposits is itself covered by a thin layer of Millstone Grit, rather as a glaze might cover an earthware bowl. Both rocks emerge from the ground, becoming visible a short distance north of the A 465 road. Here, seemingly empty moorlands rise steadily to their 1800 - 2000 feet, (c. 550 - 615m), high-points before terminating in a series of sudden and dramatic scarps which are the coalfield's true edge: Beyond lies the gentler Old Red Sandstone landscape of the Usk Valley and E. Powys. Rising moorlands force rain-bearing south-westerly winds upwards, causing heavy precipitation and creating a 'rain-shadow' for areas beyond. The upper valleys, for example, have a rainfall of c. 60 inches per annum, in striking contrast with c. 20 inches at Abergavenny, only ten miles or so distant but 700 feet lower.

Settlements tended to be sited on the coal and iron-bearing seams, any to the north of this line being usually associated with quarrying. The coal basin and its seams dipped southwards causing Millstone Grit, beneath which no coal lay, to become the colliers' 'Farewell Rock'. On the moors this hard quartzite material forms rock-scatters and thin acidic soil: Only where there are limestone extrusions is the soil sweeter, particularly when these were worked for agricultural-lime. Sweet grass attracts grazing animals, whose subsequent manuring also tends to improve soil.

A striking feature of this region is the profusion of swallow-holes, i.e. funnel-shaped depressions often of considerable diameter and depth, formed by collapsing subterranean limestone caverns and watercourses. Beneath this rolling landscape lies 'Agen Allwedd', the longest cave system yet discovered in Europe, still being explored and extended. In the heart of the moors is another celebrated cave, perhaps an outlier of the main series. This small cavern, formerly known as 'Big Stable' has a legendary association with the local uprising of 1839 thus gaining its present title of 'The Chartists' Cave'.

THE COMING OF INDUSTRY

The rapid industrial development of this region was the outcome of European Wars during the 18th and 19th centuries. This was not a gradual process; even though Merthyr Tydfil was already in existence, other iron towns were created almost overnight. Some small-scale exploitation of local iron-stone and coal had probably occurred since prehistoric times; traces of Upper Sirhowy Valley coal discovered at Blaenllynfi Castle, near Bwlch in the Usk Valley, tends to confirm this.

In the post-mediaeval period coal was certainly being obtained from the outcrop by lowland farmers, both for domestic use and to fire primitive lime kilns erected along the northern scarp. Trackways bear names possibly connected with this activity, e.g. 'Pen rhiw calch', i.e. 'Head of the limestone track/slope'. By the 18th Century local iron-stone was also being transported by pack-horse or mule to both Brecon and Llanelly (Clydach Gorge, nr. Gilwern) forges as well as to an early works at Pont-gwaith-yr-hiarn in the upper Sirhowy Valley. The establishment of far larger works during the latter part of the century brought about a massive increase in demand.

TREES AND CHARCOAL

Although early furnaces were charcoal fired, hand or water-powered bellows providing blast, their demands did not bring about an entire stripping of tree-cover. Some evidence exists for tree-plantations coppiced to provide charcoal, but large new works used only coke: Most trees would be felled to provide roof supports for levels and pits. Clydach Gorge woodlands, the oldest naturally-regenerated beech-woods in Wales, were saved only because the local forge was replaced by the Clydach Ironworks, coke-fired from its inception. Rich woodlands in the lowland areas were felled to supply timber, with a consequent detrimental effect upon landscapes. In return iron-masters from the hills, by purchasing lowland estates, did much to re-establish these areas.

The remoteness and isolation of the hill-districts and their inhabitants, inhibited any local exploitation of its vast potential. Most of the region formed part of large estates whose owners, receiving very little income, were happy to re-lease or sell. Theophilus Jones, writing of lands at Llanmarch near the Clydach Gorge, stated:

'The Duke of Beaufort, the proprietor, receives from these and other mines near £2000 each year, yet 20 years ago they were not worth £20 annually'.

Even those who were not tenants seemed totally ignorant of the wealth under their feet, and were either persuaded to sell cheaply or coerced into so-doing: Simply by establishing a navvy encampment nearby could soon strip a farm of its possessions and force its sale. Only at Glang-rwyne in the Usk Valley was there a Welsh-owned forge but it worked iron produced by English entrepreneurs. These individuals, aware of developments at Ironbridge and elsewhere, were drawn by the riches lying under the Monmouth and Glamorgan hills. Furnaces sprang up along the outcrop; Merthyr Tydfil had produced iron at least since mediaeval times, but now five great works were to be established, one of them becoming the largest industrial plant in the world. Iron works and associated new towns were created at Blaenavon, Nantyglo, Beaufort, Ebbw Vale, Sirhowy, Tredegar, Rhymney and Hirwaun. With amazing speed the once-green valleys were furnace-blackened, ancient farms and woodlands disappeared, and long ranks of housing began to spread along the moorland edge.

DESPOLIATION

The vast quantities of waste produced by the iron industry were at first tipped to create level areas for industry: River courses were altered and raised; most upper-valley floors are higher than they were in their natural state. Eventually enormous quantities of coal-pit and iron-works waste would be tipped wherever possible, little attention being paid to established settlement or the environment. Later, cable haulage would carry waste high onto mountain sides, a practice which would cause the Aberfan disaster, when a huge spoil heap slid to engulf school and houses. For nearly two hundred years white-hot molten slag was poured over what would become the 1992 Garden Festival - Wales site. Although most has been removed the 'Bluffs', a central feature, is solidified furnace-waste. Even at Merthyr Tydfil, where the Taff Valley was relatively wide, slag tipping produced dramatic results:

'Merthyr Tydfil is situated in the uppermost part of Glamorgan and lies between rough, bleak, mountains besides heaps of cinders which rise to an immense height. These heaps have been formed by the accumulation of refuse matter thrown out by the mines and furnaces. Railway embankments compared with these tips are mere pygmies. The great heat from the cinders causes them to smoulder for many years. In the evening they may be studied because of the flames of various hues caused by the burning of the sulphur which is emitted from the minerals. Many of these tips which have become cold and consolidated have been built upon.'

EXPLOITATION

Iron-stone and coal were obtained originally through 'patching', i.e. small-scale open-casting of the outcrop. Varying from small hollows to quarry-like faces, these workings created the pock-marked landscape once a feature of the region. Trenching and water-scouring methods were also employed; 'Scwrfa', now a district of Tredegar, derives its name from 'scouring-place', indicating the use of river water to wash overburden from seams.

When such surface output could no longer cope with demand, drift-mines or levels were driven into the hillsides to gain richer seams. Iron-stone was 'mine' and those who dug for it 'miners'; coal-hewers were 'coal-iers' hence 'colliers'. Underground workers were considered inferior to those who made iron, a fact indicated by a difference in pay.

The working out of surface deposits together with ever-increasing demands, meant that deeper seams had to be reached. In 1806, near Sirhowy Ironworks on the Duke of Beaufort's land, 'Duke's Pit' was sunk; at 100 feet (c. 33m.) in depth, it was the first pit in Wales.

Early pits were often operated by horse-whin, a simple horizontal windlass which was to be superseded by balance pits. This efficient system consisted of two 'cages' or 'bonds' connected by chain passing over a braked drum. Each cage was fitted with a large water tank; when the uppermost was filled it became heavy enough to lift the lower cage plus its load. At pit-bottom the lower tank would be emptied and the upper filled. Shafts tended to be sited on hill-sides enabling water to drain down a sloping adit to the river. Some of these stone-arched discharge points may still be seen.

Water-balance was not restricted to pits; at Blaenavon Works furnace-charging materials were raised by this method. Similarly, at Gilwern Hill's 'Tumble' Quarry supplying the same works, stone was so-lifted to the tramroad via a rock-cut shaft. Both shaft and associated feeder/discharge channels are still in good condition.

This was a wet area and as mining operations expanded so did the need for adequate drainage. Natural southward tilting of the strata meant that any heading following its line became flooded. Most early levels drove E - W into the seams, cutting upward to allow water to drain away to the entrance. (This also eased the task of horses pulling-out loaded trams). Later steam, then electrically driven pumps would be employed to drain difficult areas.

Seams were often too low for a horse or pony to enter and so girls and boys were employed to move trams to and from higher roofed headings. Early levels and pits might produce a combination of coal, iron-stone and fire-clay, all of which could occur in adjacent seams. Originally, what is now the 'Big Pit' mining museum at Blaenavon exploited iron-stone and fire-clay changing as coal demand increased. Gradually coal production, mainly to supply furnaces, began to take precedence over that of iron.

Furnaces could not consume all the coal now being produced and a search began for other markets, eventually making South Wales renowned throughout the world. Outlets already existed in rural Hereford, Brecon and Radnor-Shires which were supplied by pack-animals or cart. Indeed, the 1797 - 1800 Brecon Canal seems to have been intended more to monopolize this trade than to carry iron to Newport, but the original scheme for a circle of three canals connected to a canalised River Wye came to nought. In spite of this set-back coal and limestone did move along canal and tramroads to points-of-sale, causing prices to fall dramatically. *'All the world comes to Brecon for its coal'*, claimed one proud townsman. Other tramroads were constructed into the rural areas: In 1829 fifteen tons of the first Blaenavon coal to reach Hereford city were distributed to its poor by Ironmaster Hill.

IRON FURNACES AND FORGES

Stone-built, fire-clay lined furnaces, gave way to massive structures where greater heat and higher production was achieved by forced blast: A change from cold to hot blast made output soar. By being constructed against a bank, furnaces could be top-fed with a mixture of coke, iron and lime-stone.

Coke was originally made in 'clamps', i.e. earth-covered heaps, before the introduction of coke-ovens: Iron-stone was also roasted in special kilns to burn off impurities before entering the furnace:

'Monmouthshire Merlin' 5 December 1829.

'On Thursday 29th ult, a mine burner belonging to the Sirhowy Company, by the name of William Walter, whilst in the act of emptying his barrow of mine into the kiln below, fell into it and although his fellow workmen were on the spot they could afford him no assistance as the clinker broke that was on the surface where he fell when he was instantly completely hidden by the burning materials. On Saturday some of his calcined bones were taken out of the kiln.'

As the heavier iron melted it dropped into the hearth or 'bosh'. Impurities fused with melted limestone formed a liquid scum on the metal surface. When smelting was complete this slag was tapped off before the white-hot metal flowed into sand moulds. Large channels or 'sows' had numerous smaller 'pigs' projecting on either side and so 'pig-iron' gained its name. Slag was sometimes poured into rectangular moulds to form revetment blocks for such as river banks.

Cast or 'grey' iron was brittle and of limited practical use. In early times this might be re-heated, pounded and folded, under water-powered trip hammers to create 'wrought' iron, a process which removed impurities and created a far stronger molecular formation. In later ironworks this was achieved by 'puddling and rolling'.

Puddling was a process by which grey iron was re-heated in a special reverberatory, i.e. top-fired, furnace. Here it would be stirred by the puddler, using long iron tools frequently cooled in cold water. Eventually the iron 'came to nature', i.e rather glutinous and lumpy, allowing the puddler to form it into large balls of c. 30 - 40 kgs. in weight. These would then be shaped into blooms under trip hammers before being passed through rollers. The resulting bars would be cut into suitable lengths for sale. The work was heavy, exhausting and dangerous:

'Children are especially likely to suffer since the hard work must leave them exhausted and unable to move out of danger. In 1844 a 12 year-old was crushed to death by rollers at Plymouth works. Since those working the rollers had to run up to eleven miles in each shift the accident does not seem surprising.'

LIMESTONE

Extensive limestone quarries were developed along the edge of the coal basin, where this rock outcropped. Trefil Quarries, near Tredegar, not only supplied those works but also Ebbw Vale, Beaufort and Rhymney: When exhausted, other quarries were opened some distance north, overlooking the Crawnon Valley. In 1938 the establishment of the Richard Thomas Steelworks at Ebbw Vale necessitated re-opening these quarries and building a new railway line: this utilised much of the 1793 'Trefil Rail Road' route along which limestone had travelled to Beaufort and Ebbw Vale furnaces.

Many other quarries were opened-up, amongst the most dramatic being Morlais, near Merthyr; Gilwern Hill, (SO 242 127), north of Blaenavon; and Darren Cilau (SO 195 155), above Llangattock. This latter quarry supplied Nantyglo Ironworks via 'Bailey's Tramroad', the route of which, around the scarp edge near Brynmawr, provides one of the best scenic drives and walks in South Wales.

FROM IRON TO STEEL

The introduction of the Bessemer process enabled iron to be converted into steel thus ousting wrought-iron. Local iron-stone, with its high sulphur content, proved unsuitable and for a time it seemed likely that local works would close. However, there was to be a reprieve when the 'Gilchrist-Thomas' method of treating local ores for Bessemer use was developed at Blaenavon. This gave a further lease of life but, as local deposits were worked-out, more and more foreign ores were imported. Eventually, for economic reasons, several works were re-sited near ports and others closed. Shortly after the 1914 - 18 War iron and steel-making had all but ceased throughout the region.

TRANSPORT AND COMMUNICATIONS

Oxen had been the common draft-animal on many farms but the horse, mule and ass were the prime-movers of early industry. Fodder was always a problem and vast quantities had to be imported from rural districts. Experimentation with new pastures on valley sides proved that, when drained and treated with lime and basic slag, these were capable of producing heavier crops of grass and grain than many farms in the lowlands:

'But the iron-masters have improved the sterility of the lands which are now as prolific as many counties that are devoted to the cultivation of grain and the growth of cattle'.

The normal early unit of trade was the 'dozen', the quantity which could be carried by 12 horses or mules, i.e. c. 36 cwts. (1812 kgs.) Transport improvements were inspired by the desire to move ever-greater loads and maximize the efficiency of expensive-to-maintain draft animals. A mule or horse could carry 3 cwts (151 kgs.) on its back, but if pulling a cart could move a ton. If that cart ran along a smooth tramroad the load could be four or five tons; if attached to a canal barge, the same horse could move twenty tons. Lower costs meant greater profits and the development of steam locomotion was principally to provide a cheaper, untiring and reliable alternative. However, without draft animals no early industry could have been established on the Monmouth and Glamorgan hills.

'Hereford Times', Saturday 26 October 1839.

'A locomotive steam engine intended to ply on Messrs. Baileys' tramroad from Nantyglo to Llangattock passed through this town (Abergavenny) on Tuesday last, on its way to the former place. This piece of machinery whilst remaining in the town attracted general observation. It came from the Old Park Foundry at Wednesbury, Staffs., and was manufactured by Lloyd, Foster and Co., the well known and eminent makers. The engine is called 'Sampson' and is of 40 h.p. and appears a handsome piece of mechanism being calculated to perform feats of drawing burthens in its train which some time back seemed impossible. Its weight alone is 8 tons and, including carriage and tender, is upward of 19 tons.

CANALS AND TRAMROADS

The ever-increasing trade in iron, coal and steel changed Cardiff and Newport from unimportant villages into large sea-ports. From Merthyr Tydfil the Taff Valley facilitated the construction of a canal directly to Cardiff; Richard Trevethick's steam locomotive of 1804, the first in the world, operated between Penydarren Works and this waterway. Later the canal was to be superseded by Brunel's Taff Valley Railway.

In Monmouthshire long and expensive tramroad links were built to connect various works with the 1794 Crumlin Canal, and its 1796 Pontypool spur, to Newport. The Brecon Canal was not fully open until 1812 and mule trains were still carrying some coal and iron from Beaufort and Nantyglo. From Tredegar ran the celebrated Sirhowy Tramroad, some twenty-four miles in length, directly to 'Tredegar Wharf' at Newport. Along it travelled some of the first passenger vehicles in the world and its success inspired the building of the Stockton and Darlington Railway on which Stephenson's 'Rocket' would run. Interestingly, the first steam locomotive on the 'Sirhowy' would also be a Stephenson design.

Monmouthshire Merlin' - 26 December 1829. (Reporting on the first run of the 'St. David').

'The engine did start from the (Tredegar) works early in the morning but, unfortunately, at one of the tram-road crossings the wheels got off the tram-plates which caused a detention of some hours, and in coming through Tredegar Park (Newport) the chimney was carried away by the branch of a tree and in consequence did not arrive at Newport until the evening. The engine is very compact, the carriage consists of six wheels on which is the boiler and the machinery behind which the engineer stands to work it. There is also a carriage attached carrying the coke. The engine is about 8 horse-power and brought down 53 tons of iron besides its own weight making a load altogether of about 80 tons at a rate of 6 m.p.h. and with some ease without forcing the engine …she went at the rate of 10 m.p.h. with nothing attached …it is generally believed that the engine will answer the purpose intended and that horses will be put out of request.'

The Usk Valley, passing close to the coalfield's northern edge, made possible the construction of the Brecon-Newport Canal and its associated tramroad links. Many of these are now footpaths, one of the most dramatic being that section of Benjamin Hall's 'Brinore' between Trefil and Talybont-on-Usk.

RAILWAYS

Canals and tramroads ceased to be economic with the building of railways in the mid-century. Apart from valley lines, the two major routes through the area were those of the Abergavenny-Tredegar-Merthyr (Later L.M.S.) and the Newport-Dowlais-Talybont, (eventually G.W.R.). Long stretches of their road-beds now form footpaths.

THE PEOPLE

Nature had provided all the materials for iron-making, but in a sparsely-populated region far from the sea. The new industries were labour intensive in themselves but also spawned supporting crafts and trades. There was demand for builders, masons, carpenters, glaziers, quarrymen and carters. Mule and horse drivers were required, as were blacksmiths and farriers: Tinsmiths, grocers, publicans and a dozen other trades were also essential to make the new industries and towns work. The ironmasters built their furnaces, laid out rows of cottages, and waited.

Some of the skills necessary would have existed amongst the indigenous population and local entrepreneurs had their own gangs moving from place to place. But the new developments were vast; Tredegar town and works, for example, were decreed, planned and largely completed within a year. Furnaces arose near levels which would supply them with coal and iron-stone. Alongside the works, grid-patterned streets and a town square were laid out, together with the first rows of houses. Soon a populous town and works existed where once had been only farms.

It was the same all along the outcrop; a mid-century writer, commenting on Merthyr's size stated:

'About 90 years ago Merthyr was a small village inhabited only by shepherds and farmers.'

News of the developments had spread and with it the realisation that men, women and children, were needed in large numbers to serve the industries that were making the hills an Eldorado. It was a belief which did not fade; many years later Italians would be attracted to a South Wales *'whose streets were paved with gold'*. Although skilled workers were brought in from other areas, the unskilled majority arrived from rural districts, often deserting marginal lands and subsistence-level holdings.

The new works and settlements also affected rural areas in other ways. Now began that massive demand for fodder, food-stuffs and timber which the lowlands could supply. This was an immense market and its requirements benefitted many.

At first the workforce was predominantly Welsh who came from all parts of the Principality. There are accounts of farm girls walking bare-foot from West Wales to find work; family connections still exist with what were then remote areas. As the industries developed the first arrivals would be joined by English, Scots, Irish, Italians, Spanish, Jews and others, forbears of those who live here today. Local surnames reveal how diverse were the origins of many who now consider themselves totally 'Welsh'.

Working conditions were certainly harsh but it is misleading to judge only against modern standards. This was an area of high wages, incomparably better than anything in rural districts. Money and prosperity were the prerogative of the hills, the lowlands being, in the main, places of backwardness and poverty. It is also incorrect to assume that work-people were always exploited and degraded by ruthless masters: Many of the latter were highly respected by their workers, considered to have the interests of their people at heart.

Even though the unskilled nature of much work, together with a ready supply of labour, gave employers the upper hand, there were those who tried to improve their workers' lot. Richard Crawshay of Cyfartha, apart from believing that his men should *'have beef and beer every day'*, paid them in coin rather than company money. A library was to be established at Dowlais, whilst Tredegar Iron Company organized a free school for workers' children, over seventy of whom are said to have regularly attended. It has become fashionable to denigrate these Ironmasters although many were highly-regarded by their own workforces. Conditions in this region were no worse, and often very much better, than was the norm; some masters appearing quite philanthropic in the light of their times. Even the much-maligned 'Truck' system, by which workers were paid in company money, acceptable only in company shops or heavily discounted elsewhere, was not acceptable to all proprietors. In April 1830, Sir Charles Morgan of Tredegar, speaking in the House of Commons vigorously opposed the system stating *'it was of great hardship to workingmen and independent traders'*. He begged that the practice be stopped so that *'the full payment of a workman's stipulated wage in money was made without deduction, evasion or delay, and in no other way whatsoever'.*

The lot of many workers would seem to have been acceptable, sometimes good, as long as they were not old, injured or sick, conditions for which few societies made provision. Those able to save, perhaps joining one of the burgeoning Friendly Societies could more readily survive times of strike or injury. Even though working conditions were harsh and dangerous there was leisure-time, one day a week and part of every other day normally being free. Large numbers of working men, with time on their hands, provided ready audiences for those advocating social and political change. Ever-present was the fear that sickness, injury or poverty would lead to the dreaded Workhouse.

'Hereford Times', Saturday 18 June 1836.

'A melancholy and fatal accident at Tredegar Works.

On Monday evening last a pitman by the name of William Williams employed at 'Ty'n yr heol' balance pit at the above works, in attempting to place a tram upon the carriage, by some means forced it to the wrong side of the pit and in an instant both tram and himself were precipitated to the bottom, a depth of about 90 yards (c. 83m.), so as to cause the poor fellow's instantaneous death. He was found in a state of mutilation too appalling to be described. William Williams was a native of Llandeilo, Carms. and was a married man of about 51 years of age and had not been employed more than 12 months in the Tredegar Iron Works. He left a widow and 12 children. The circumstance of their being in a strange country renders their situation truly depressing'.

Housing conditions were standard for the period, often far better than those of the country-side. Rows of thick-walled, small-windowed and stone-tiled dwellings were erected, certain elements of their design deriving from rural vernacular. Most of these have now been demolished, and those remaining very-much altered. Larger, double-fronted, houses at the end of each row were those of better paid, skilled, workers.

Then, as now, the condition of a house could tell much of its occupants' character. Edwin Roberts, visiting Merthyr in 1852 described what must have been typical of the area at that time:

'As the doors are generally open the passing glance within shows tolerable exactitude of thrifty or prodigal taste of the owners. In some are substantial furniture, or pictures on the walls and a range of shining culinary utensils on the mantelshelf harmonize pleasantly with the clean delf (sic) and a cupboard full of crockery and glass in the corner. The gorgeously emblazoned set of trays vies with the American clock with the newest face.

There are exceptions to the rule. Before dirty doors and greasy windows you observe that the pavement is broken or the earth dug in holes, offering a facility for the manufacture of mud-pies if the weather is favourable. The floor within is not to be distinguished in colour from the mildewed and blotchy walls. On one you observe no ornate attempts, and on the other the scantiest of rickety furniture. A repulsive barrenness reigns within and a fenderless fireplace is fitter for a hovel than a house. Women, unclean, untidy, slatternly of personal attire show that their souls have been crushed and degraded by brutality and the example of pater-nal vicious habits which have reached their leprous lengths to them. Foetid pools stand about, the cinders are flung before the doors and other refuse cast amongst them which ferments and taints the air.'

The same visitor described the filthy conditions prevailing in some privies, the earth-closets often set into a walled bank. It was the dumping of this 'night-soil' near water-sources which probably caused the various cholera epidemics which ravaged the area.

Another writer, commenting on the same problem stated:

'The majority of houses have no privies, where there is such a thing it is merely a hole in the ground with no drainage.'

Yet again it must be remembered that such conditions would have been considered normal in those rural areas from which many had come, only becoming totally inadequate when large numbers lived in close proximity. Even the Tredegar Company's plans for a well-laid out town broke down under weight of numbers. Cholera, its causes misunderstood, was inevitable in such conditions.

Water supplies came from 'spouts', i.e. iron tubes driven into spring-lines and from which water gushed continuously. It was a woman's task to fetch water and spouts became social centres and places of gossip. A newcomer to the region recorded:

'The water comes from spouts in the mountainside round which between 10 - 60 women are constantly to be seen from about six in the morning to midnight, and which are great centres of gossip and scandal'.

GIRLS AT WORK

Single girls and widows worked in the various industries although this was not customary for married women. The younger and more attractive were always in danger of being seduced by overseers and masters. Robert Thomson Crawshay, a later owner of Cyfartha, Merthyr, is believed to have established many small businesses in the town by settling sums of money on girls pregnant by him. Obviously well-aware of such temptations a visitor to Cyfartha wrote:

'We at first approached the machinery where a huge hammer crushed masses of limestone into fragments and was attended by two girls, as fine grown and elegantly-limbed young creatures as I had ever seen. The hard work attended to the development of the frame for handsomer arms and finer busts could not be met with. With heavy hammers they broke the large pieces and with spades fed the trough where the great hammer was at work. They scarce laid down their work when we passed and for all the grime and dust of their labour hardly hid the pleasing lineaments of their young faces, calm and modest as they were with gentle eyes of a bluish tinge, their brown hair only partly confined by a kerchief, I thought I had never seen anything so soft and charming in its retiring femininity, in contrast as it was with the other accessories of the enormous mass of physical and machine labour around them. The noise of the hammers, the shouting of the men and the roar

of the blast-furnaces, the sounding of pistons and the hissing of steam and the most infernal din and aspect of the whole, they retrieved the whole from whatever there was repulsive in its aspect.

There are seductions enough, no doubt, and I was told that the young masters played the part of so many sultans and that there were sultanas that were not always submissive to the royal kerchief, but more reasons were given for their command over their victims than I need not here set down. Given the peculiar relationship between them it is not hard to imagine with what success. To be virtuous under difficulties is not always possible. An ill-informed, rudely-cultured girl, whatever may be her innate qualities, may be pardoned for submitting to overtures made to her with threats, like promise of higher pay and lighter work, or more brutal and business-like manner of virtue bought or sold, or a menace to be dismissed from nearby employ; these and a score of other reasons may be given and all this may be traced to the system of forcing girls to work in these places at all. It is not their fault and I conscientiously exonerate them'.

Young girls were exposed to risks other than moral. Men women and children all worked in dangerous conditions which were considered quite acceptable and normal. Rules concerning health and safety are a recent innovation; at that time accidents were common-place.

'Burns and scalds from hot metal are frequent. At the Dowlais Works five men died when part of a furnace collapsed and some six months later six more died when a boiler exploded'.

Such bare statistics make no mention of the dependants left to fend for themselves.

THE NEW TOWNS

Tredegar was fortunate in that its original central area was planned, providing a grid-pattern of wide streets. Others grew randomly and conditions at Merthyr must have been typical. During the 1830's and 40's its newspaper complained:

'There is a wretched state of the street and a want of gas-lights. The passenger is in constant danger of dipping his foot in a puddle or to be tripped-up, or if he escapes, suffer the greater calamity of falling into a cellar through rotten trapdoors, or insecure iron gratings. The inhabitants prefer to walk in the streets'.

'On dark nights it is positively dangerous to traverse the streets. The uncertain fitful light of the blast-furnaces only serves to render the darkness visible'.

The Glamorgan and Merthyr Gazette also issued some tongue-in-cheek advice to visitors:

'To strangers and others: After dark make sure you are walking in the middle of the street and by no account on what is termed the 'flat pavement' lest you fall in holes or sink in the mud at the sides. Carry a lanthorn and wear clogs or boots for to sweep or light the streets forms no part of municipal requirements at Merthyr. Should you visit the spacious market-place be careful lest, as was the case with the damsel from Rhymney, you fall up to your middle into the pits considerately left for the reception of blood offal and filth of the slaughter-house and for the pigs thereof. N.B., there is great encouragement to lovers of good cheer to visit Merthyr as the beer and gin shops abound and are kept open night and day for the accommodation of gentry

and others who soar above the vulgar prejudices of teetotallers'.

However, the town altered little; even by 1854 when George Borrow passed through he was appalled by what he saw:

'I went through a filthy slough and up a street where dirty lanes branched off on either side and passed throngs of dirty-looking people talking clamorously'.

CHAPEL AND PUBLIC HOUSE

Chapels, beer and gin-houses were numerous in all iron-towns, being social centres and places of great influence; regular attendance at one or other was considered a good indication of attitudes and standards. Churches were considered preserves of masters and others in authority; chapels for workers and their families. Places of worship tended to be full for every service, especially during times of trouble or infection; Nonconformist Sunday Schools provided the only means of education for many. It is impossible to over-emphasize the chapels' contribution during those times.

In 1848 there were 136 beer-houses and gin-shops in Merthyr alone with another 100 in adjoining Dowlais. Drunkenness was an accepted fact of the age throughout society, and 'signing the pledge' i.e. promising upon the Bible never to drink, became an important weapon in the chapels' armoury. The heat of furnace and foundry created enormous thirsts and it was common for workers to consume gallons of beer during each shift. Young boys, known as 'fetchers', ran between public house and works bearing jugs filled 'on the slate', part of the 'old score' to be settled on pay-days. The 'Long Draw', as pay-days became known, was often held in public houses, the four or so weeks between each being considered essential to keep the works producing: Many workers, with money in their pockets, would stay drunk until it was all spent. Publicans bribed pay-agents to arrive late, while wives thronged anxiously outside, often begging their men for money essential for food: Heavily salted soups were often made freely available to drinkers at such times. Public houses were ideal places for the dissemination of radical ideas that would feed on imaginary or real discontent. Many were becoming aware that society must change and took up avidly the new concepts of 'Chartism' which began to sweep through the coalfield.

'THE BRITISH REVOLUTION'

In this tumultuous, crowded and lawless, region political agitators found ready listeners. The recent French Revolution still exercised many minds; there were those who believed that Britain would not change for the better until it followed the same course of action. Many working men were encouraged to believe that this was the only way by which their conditions would be improved. However, Chartist ideals were not accepted by all.

Few other industrial regions of the kingdom seemed as potentially explosive as that of the iron-towns. The Merthyr Riots of 1831, and the hanging of local leader 'Dic Penderyn' created a martyr, whilst preparing the ground for what would follow. Strangely, even though his town became a hotbed of Chartism, awareness of Dic Penderyn's fate may have been the reason why none of its vociferous Chartists played a part in the actual rising.

By 1836, a group of liberal-minded gentlemen, anxious to improve social conditions, set-up the 'London Workingmen's Association' which, the following year, issued its celebrated 'Workers' Charter'. The fact that five of its demands eventually became part of our political system indicates either the Charter's impact or the inevitability of Reform. Basically working-men, women were never considered, wanted to be able to vote their own state-funded M.P.'s into Parliament. It was a just request and recognised as such by widely-differing sections of the community.

Chartist orator Henry Vincent, of undoubted revolutionary beliefs, amongst which was the destruction of the aristocracy, inspired the coalfield. Soon three local leaders appeared: John Frost, a Newport draper; Zephania Williams, colliery & property-owner, mineral agent turned publican: and William Jones, watchmaker of Pontypool. All three were prosperous middle-class men. The movement spread rapidly with lodges being established in many public houses. Interestingly, none are said to have existed in Tredegar whose Ironmaster, Sam Homfray, was held in high esteem. Chartism was strongly opposed by Nonconformist chapels and their members: However, in an area where 'Scotch Cattle' had already enforced their own particular labour-codes through violence and intimidation, few workers could be seen to openly-resist.

From the outset Chartist supporters divided themselves into those desiring peaceful change and others who advocated force. By the late-Autumn of 1839 'Physical Force' concepts had prevailed. Chartism's 'Great Petition Of A Million Signatures' had been rejected by government with the discovery that many had been forged. 'Moral Force' was spurned and armed struggle planned: Chartists would rise in open revolution throughout the country; the signal being the seizure of Newport by Monmouthshire men.

By November 1839 a secret army had been formed and on Sunday the 3rd three great columns began their march. Although thousands took part believing that this was the only way to change society for the better, many reluctant supporters fled to seek refuge wherever they could: It has been postulated that severed human bones discovered in the Chartists' Cave near Tredegar may have been those of suspected informers. Alan Pinkerton, later to establish the celebrated U.S. Detective Agency, possibly acted as a Government agent, claiming to have taken part in the actual march.

On Monday morning Sirhowy and Nantyglo marchers met at Risca where they waited for the

Pontypool contingent. News reached Newport in the small hours enabling its tiny garrison to be alerted. Marching on without the Pontypool men, at approximately eight o'clock John Frost entered the town at the head of a well-armed and ordered column. The Westgate Hotel, where Mayor Thomas Phillips had taken post, came under determined attack. Only after Chartists had broken into the building, and several defenders including the Mayor, had fallen wounded, was the continent of twenty-eight soldiers 'kept out of sight so not to inflame the mob', brought into action. Three volleys of musket-fire were enough; moments later the square was empty apart from nine wounded and dying amidst a litter of abandoned weapons. Thus ended 'The British Revolution'.

Eventually captured and tried, Frost, Williams and Jones were sentenced to be hanged but, with the country in such unrest, this was commuted to transportation to Tasmania. In 1854, when transportation ceased, all three were granted pardons. Only Frost was eventually to return home, finally settling at Stapleton, near Bristol, rather than Newport whose citizens were less than welcoming.

An apt epitaph was uttered by one of the Westgate's defending soldiers. Following the attack's failure two Chartists discovered hiding in one of its rooms were placed with the soldiers who were eating breakfast:

'The miserable fellows were wet and looked wistfully at the bread and cheese the soldiers were eating. A soldier of the 45th Regt. observing their hungry appearance, presented his share of the food saying 'Eat this, my bucks, and make yourselves comfortable for, by God 'tis well if you eat another morsel after this morning''.

Attitudes change; history is re-written and interpreted. The few who were Newport's heroes in 1839 are now considered brutal minions of an intolerant state; those who might have brought about full-scale revolution, with unknown consequences for Britain and the World, are honoured.

THE FUTURE

Before iron and steel-making ended the coal industry had become predominant, supplying many parts of the world. Even that industry went into severe decline during the 1930's when South Wales suffered tremendous poverty and hardship. By 1938, against all prevailing economic trends, the Richard Thomas Steelworks was opened in Ebbw Vale and, for the next forty years, brought prosperity to the area.

Now all steel-making has ceased and the pits have closed; valleys are becoming green again but at tremendous social cost. In an attempt to present a new image all traces of an amazing industrial heritage are being swept away; soon little will remain of the days when furnaces spewed out their iron and slag across the outcrop. Not one spoil heap will recall those times when South Wales was the iron and coal centre of the world: An incredible era has ended.

THE END

THE OUTCROP

The North-South tilt of the South Wales Coal-basin meant that rich seams of coal, iron-stone ('mine') and fire-clay 'outcropped', i.e. came to the surface along its northern edge. Here rose also the limestone of the basin itself, essential as a furnace 'flux'. Along a narrow belt of land between Hirwaun and Blaenavon was everything necessary for the production of iron in vast quantities.

At first the outcrop was 'patched', i.e. worked by means of small-scale open-cast sites which created the pock-marked landscape once so characteristic of this area. The illustration shows a typical section of the outcrop at Beaufort, near Ebbw Vale, with 'Elled' coal and associated deposits being exploited. Iron-stone and coal seams were often in proximity; the drawing reveals how close to the ground surface and readily accessible they were.

A horse-operated tramroad carries away minerals and waste; workmen cut at seams exposed on the quarry-like face. Others, using picks, shovels and wheelbarrow, clear away the overburden to reach seams beneath.

Similar early scenes could have been witnessed across the region. Later such small-scale workings could not keep up with demands which could only be met by 'levels' and pits.

The Elled Patch, Beaufort, South Wales.

DOWLAIS IRONWORKS - MERTHYR TYDFIL - 1840

George Childs was commissioned to record the Dowlais Ironworks of 1840, producing watercolours now in the possession of the Welsh Industrial & Maritime Museum, Cardiff. These paintings provide some of the very best industrial representations of their times.

Dowlais was not the largest of Merthyr's five great works, that distinction went to Cyfartha, but even so it was larger than any other then existing along the 'iron-belt'. Child's painting indicates the pall of smoke and fume overhanging the area by day; at night red furnace-glare would light the skies from Hirwaun to Blaenavon.

Banks of furnaces stand against higher ground upon which were the charging platforms: Furnaces were fed from above, slag and molten iron tapped-off at their base. Two men and a woman work in the foreground, others, perhaps at leisure between shifts, look out over the scene. Had they glanced to their right, down the valley, they would have seen the neighbouring 'Penydarren' works with 'Plymouth' a short distance beyond. Looking in the direction of the Brecon Beacons, before them would have risen the smoke and flame of Crawshay's 'Cyfartha', then the greatest industrial plant in existence, together with that of its associated 'Ynysfach' works. Merthyr Tydfil was, in truth, the iron-making capital of the world.

In the immediate foreground is a plateway upon which is a tram of the type commonly used throughout the region. Horses and other trams may be seen in the far distance but, by this time, such draught-animals were losing their supremacy to steam locomotion.

GLANGRWYNE FORGE - BRECONSHIRE

Situated c. 2 kms. N. of Gilwern, on the Usk's northern bank, Glangrwyne Forge was established by a Welshman, Walter Watkins, who would also build the 1790 Penycae Furnace at Ebbw Vale. By 1793 the forge was owned by Messrs. Monkhouse and Fothergill, joint-owners of Sirhowy Works, near where Tredegar would be built. According to Richard Colt Hoare, 'they bring their coking coal and pig-iron, which is hammered into bars and conveyed by land-carriage to Newport and other markets, but the concern is not on a very extensive scale'.

The water-wheels illustrated were powered by the Grwyne Brook flowing into a forge-pond retained by the wall behind. They were 'over-shot', i.e. water came from above, and levers controlling the sluices project from the forge roof. The wheels operated large trip-hammers, their counter-weighted ends are shown emerging from the building.

Other details are not so clear; the flat slab-like shapes in the foreground may represent the 'merchant bars' of wrought-iron produced by the forge. Those would have been assembled into pack-mule or other loads by means of the balance and weights alongside.

In 1794 a new rail-road, (differing from plateways in that tram wheels actually ran on top of iron rails), was constructed to connect Glangrwyne with the coalfield but, in the following year, its Usk bridge was swept away by floods. The rail-road also suffered from continual breakages and was rebuilt as a plateway.

FORGING IRON - MERTHYR TYDFIL

An early forge at Cyfartha Works, painted by J.C. Ibbetson.

'Grey' cast-iron, poured into moulds alongside the furnace, was too brittle for most practical purposes. During the early days of the industry this was re-heated and beaten under heavy 'trip' hammers making it far stronger and resilient. (The hammering caused molecules within the iron to become linked.) White-hot cast-iron 'pigs' were beaten, folded and beaten again into 'merchant bars' of wrought-iron.

The painting shows the process clearly: In the foreground is the huge hammer-beam behind which is a water-wheel providing power. Another hammer beats white-hot iron being turned and controlled by a workman. A re-heated and partially completed bar, its folds are visible, is being dragged in from the furnace.

Noteworthy is the lack of any protective clothing other than what appear to be leather aprons; all workers are in normal everyday clothes of the period. The dangers are obvious for those working with hot metal and unprotected machinery. Another element of risk was that staring at white-hot iron for long periods would damage the sight; poor vision and even blindness were endemic in this trade.

Hammer forging would, eventually, be replaced by 'puddling and rolling'. That, too, could result in terrible accidents, mutilation and blinding.

PUDDLING FURNACES - CWMBRAN

Forging cast-iron into stronger wrought-iron was to be superseded by puddling & rolling.

Bars were placed in special reverberatory furnaces which directed heat downwards from above. As it melted the iron was stirred by a 'puddler' using long iron rods frequently cooled in water. When the metal reached a glutinous consistency it was said to 'have come to nature', i.e. ready to be formed into large balls of some 30 - 40 kgs. in weight. These were then beaten under trip hammers and passed through 'shingling' rollers. The resulting bars would be cut into suitable lengths for sale.

This dangerous and exhausting employment continued until the Bessemer process of steel-making was introduced into the area. Even then, wrought-iron was often considered the better product.

'The puddler is exposed to scorching heat and light of the most dazzling brilliancy which no ordinary person could look at ...the occupation is one of great personal exertion while exposed to an intense fire that no one not accustomed to it could even approach'

(Contemporary eye-witness).

George Robertson is credited with this early Nantyglo view although there are some doubts both about this claim and its dating. It may, in fact, represent the same works a number of years later.

Nantyglo i.e. 'Coal stream' became in turn the property of two cousins, Joseph and Crawshay Bailey, nephews of Cyfartha's master Richard Crawshay. The former had, according to popular belief, 'walked barefoot from Yorkshire'. So convinced was Joseph Bailey that the British Revolution would break out here that he had Martello-type towers constructed to protect his house. Crawshay Bailey continued to maintain these structures which are still in existence. Such fears were not ill-founded; the revolution, better known as 'The Chartist Uprising', did break out on these hills but, in apparent contradiction to modern claims of oppression and hatred, no violence took place against any owner or his family.

Joseph Bailey bought an Usk Valley estate and was eventually knighted; his grandson became the first Lord Glanusk. Crawshay Bailey, known locally as 'a kindly man', was keenly interested in steam locomotion. He is immortalised by the old song:

'Crawshay Bailey had an engine,
And the engine wouldn't go,
So he pulled it on a string,
All the way to Nantyglo.

Did you ever see,
Did you ever see,
Did you ever see,
Such a funny thing before?'

CYFARTHA WORKS - MERTHYR TYDFIL

Penry Williams's painting expresses the atmosphere of Cyfartha, then the greatest single industrial plant in the world. Although Merthyr had a long tradition of iron-making - the guns of Nelson's 'Victory' are said to have been cast there - it was not until the arrival of Richard Crawshay in 1786 that it attained pre-eminence. Here he commenced improving raw iron by rolling, and built a huge water-wheel to power furnace-blast. He was a 'strict but good master' who built chapels for his workers and brought Robert Raikes, of Sunday School fame, to establish one in Merthyr.

Horses, mules and asses figure prominently in the scene, either as individual pack-animals, or in tandem on tramroads. Ranks of furnaces are lined against a bank and, nearby, is a row of puddling forges. Other forges are in the foreground, alongside a building housing water-wheel powered trip-hammers and their associated re-heating furnaces.

In 1847 his grandson William Crawshay, in an address on his renowned forebear stated *'He rode his own pony from Yorkshire to London …he sold the pony for £15 and lived on the proceeds before finding employment in an iron warehouse where he was put in charge of selling flat-irons. He was sharp enough to prevent the washerwomen stealing two for every one they purchased and so gained his master's favour! His motto was 'Activity, Integrity and Perseverance!''*

These were sentiments which applied throughout the iron-belt.

TREDEGAR IRON AND STEEL WORKS IN THE LATE 19th CENTURY

This photograph was taken on a normal working day and yet not a human being seems to be in sight. Photographic emulsions, used for glass-plate negatives, were very slow and could not easily record movement: Faint white dots indicate where some workers hesitated long enough to register. Even the smoke from chimney stacks dissipated too quickly; only a locomotive's strong steam exhaust can be seen.

Tredegar Works was the largest in Monmouthshire. Built in 1800, it was now nearing its end. The level compound had been created by tipping furnace-slag and shifting the Sirhowy River from its original course. Close to the works lies the town, with houses, shops, chapels and other buildings contouring along the hillside. For many years its postal address had been 'Tredegar Iron Works', the town being considered but an incidental part of that enterprise; it was well into the century before this changed. In the background, on the hillside, is 'Mountain Pit farm' where once stood a balance-pit, its drainage adit discharging into the river, flowing out-of-sight, in the immediate foreground. Also visible is the wooden head-gear of 'Globe Pit', between the two stacks at the right-hand side.

Furnaces, charging platforms, blast-houses, cupolas, casting-sheds and offices make up the complex. A company saddle-tank locomotive waits to take a train onto the main line; it works 'cab-up' as there would be no long inclines. The main line replaced the celebrated 'Sirhowy Tramroad' of 1805 along which Tredegar iron and coal had travelled to the docks at Newport and the markets of the world.

Today, one hundred years later, virtually nothing remains.

EARLY WORKING CONDITIONS

(From Parliamentary Papers - 'Employment of Children' - 1842.)

A 'Bell-Pit', i.e. a widening at the bottom of a primitive shaft, is shown together with its horse-whin winding system. A rope winds around a horizontal drum worked by a horse, raising and lowering the bucket shown underground. Girl surface workers move trams loaded with pit-waste or coal; men dig at a surface 'patch' of outcropped seams; a boy makes his way to work lighted by a flaring torch.

Underground another girl moves a tram. The haulage bucket in which coal, waste and workers would be transported was impossible for horses which would have eased her labour. Buckets were notoriously unstable and often snagged against rough places, plunging their occupants or contents to the bottom. The boy in charge of the whin-horse had to exercise great caution.

Later 'balance-pits' would permit deeper workings, their 'cages' enabling greater loads to be raised more rapidly and safely. For the first time ponies could be taken down a pit-shaft; mining techniques also improved with long timber-supported headings driven deeply into the seams.

MINERS DESCENDING A SHAFT

Taken from Louis Simonin's Nineteenth Century 'Underground Life', this vividly illustrates the dangers of pit-work. Although representing a Continental pit, it provides some indication of what must have prevailed earlier in this area.

Men ride down to pit-bottom standing on the rim of a timber bucket whilst steadying themselves against the shaft wall. At the landing another worker waits to pull-in the bucket with a hooked-pole. He is barefoot, as are two others. This is no exaggeration, in the Forest of Dean iron-mines during the same period, young boys were recorded as having *'thick hoof-like pads of a horny substance on feet, elbows and knees, caused by their crawling with heavy loads'*.

Broad-brimmed hats provided some protection against falling water and small debris. In this instance safety-lamps are being carried: By this time in the iron-towns, working conditions underground were, in the main, much better than is indicated here.

Even allowing for some degree of artistic licence, Simonin reveals conditions of quite incredible danger that must have been commonplace throughout the industry. During later times, when totally-different attitudes and legislation brought-about safer equipment and methods, underground work remained a very hazardous occupation.

Another illustration from Siminon's work may relate to early pits in this area by indicating how a bucket-haulage system could lead to disaster. Three buckets are shown being raised, two filled with coal and the other used to carry men. Such loads, freely swinging from side to side, often touched shaft walls and, by snagging on any projection, could either break the rope or tip out contents or occupants.

Even in later 'balance-pits' with their new system of cages there were accidents. Only when guide rails and steel ropes were introduced did these become less-frequent. Even then 'over-winding' could pull a cage completely out of its shaft to smash against headgear. The 'winder' in charge of the haulage engine was required to be highly-skilled and careful.

WATER-BALANCE PITS

As easily-accessible surface deposits of coal and iron-stone became worked-out, or insufficient to meet ever-increasing demand, it was necessary to reach deeper and richer deposits. Upper seams could be worked by drifts or 'levels' driven into the hillsides, but lower seams required pit-shafts.

Horse-whin systems of winding, i.e. raising and lowering, gave way to water-balance. This method was simple and efficient, requiring only a reliable water supply and good pit-bottom drainage. Shafts were not very deep and tended to be sited on hillsides; a sloping underground adit enabling waste water to drain away, usually to the river.

A chain, passing over a braked-wheel, was attached to two 'cages', each equipped with a large water-tank. When the upper-most tank was filled and the band-brake released this provided sufficient weight to lift the lower cage plus its load. At pit-bottom the full tank would be emptied, water draining away down the adit, while the now upper cage-tank would be filled.

Water-balance was used other than in pits, both in quarries and ironworks. Only its relative slowness and inability to cope with ever-higher production, caused it to be superseded by steam-winding.

50

UNDERGROUND - THE YARD LEVEL, TREDEGAR

The first level driven in Tredegar was the 'Cwm Rhos' of 1800, followed a year later by the 'Yard Level'. This was so-named because its entrance was in the works yard, near the furnaces; indeed, its main purpose was to provide them with coking-coal and iron-stone.

The stone-arched roof indicates that the heading ran initially through unstable, even man-made, ground. The well-laid courses suggest that these may have been laid in the open-air before being covered over, i.e., as an outer extension to the original entrance. This method was often employed where pit-waste or furnace slag was intended to be tipped; in this instance furnace platforms had been constructed above.

The plateway, along which horses drew trams loaded with coal and iron-stone, was remarkably well-preserved when this photograph was taken in the 1970's. Wrought-iron deteriorates more slowly than steel and the L-shaped plates of this material are clearly in good condition. Headings were rarely larger than was absolutely necessary, usually only of sufficient size for a horse and loaded trams. In later pits and levels 'man-holes' would be cut at intervals providing shelter when a 'journey' of trams passed. When these were being pulled by an engine-powered steel haulage-rope men had to get out of the way very quickly.

Levels were driven slightly upward so that water would drain away to the entrance - a drainage channel lies to the one side. Similarly this also aided horses pulling out heavily-loaded trams.

UNDERGROUND - PLATEWAY TRAM, THE YARD LEVEL

Deep inside the Yard Level, Tredegar, this well-preserved plateway tram was discovered in the 1970's. Even though all timber work had rotted away, its iron-work was in a very good state, even the 'knife-edged' wheels revolving freely on their axles. The tram now forms part of the Welsh Industrial & Maritime Museum collection.

Horses were unable to enter workings where the roof was low and so, at first, trams had to be man-handled, often by boys and girls with a hooked chain attached to their belts. The normal, and cheapest, method of underground lighting was the candle, supplied by the workers themselves; several candle-remnants were found in the vicinity.

Much water had gathered at this place. In spite of all attempts at drainage large pools of filthy water through which animals and humans would have to pass formed wherever the ground sank, or a low place became unavoidable. In this area of high rainfall drainage underground was always a major problem. Many coal and iron-stone faces, and the headings leading to them, had water falling from their roofs: No waterproof clothing was available; when a pit or level was wet, so were its workers.

UNDERGROUND - CUTTING COAL, NUMBER 7 PIT, SIRHOWY

A late Nineteenth Century photograph filled with interesting detail. Amazingly 'open' flash, i.e. ignited magnesium powder was used, a sure sign that the seam was completely gas-free. Nowadays it would be quite illegal to take any possible means of ignition, even a battery-powered watch, into a pit.

Two colliers, both attired in very clean clothes for the photograph, use picks to undercut the coal face. This would be propped as the cut deepened, then knocked away so that the coal would fall. Anything other than large lump was unsaleable, usually thrown into 'gobs', i.e. voids, or onto surface tips. Even then it would be regarded as coal-owner's property; gathering it was an offence. As the face advanced abandoned workings would collapse, often causing subsidence on the surface above.

The fireman, his boots and lower trouser-legs wet - he had walked through some wet part of the pit - holds his two badges of office, namely the Davy lamp with which he would have tested for gas together with the stick used to sound stall and heading roofs. Any hollowness would be a warning of imminent collapse; roof-falls were a common cause of death and injury underground.

The colliers work by the light of 'ball and peg' oil lamps, one stuck into the coal face, the other in the floor. The work-place or stall is 'packed' on either side, stone extracted from seams and elsewhere being used to provide additional roof support. Props are of local deciduous timber, rather than the imported pine then becoming common throughout the coalfield. Every collier provided his own set of tools; leaning to one side are the essential shovels, sledge hammer and axe, the latter used to shape and notch the timber props.

Although situated in the Sirhowy Valley, but a short distance from Tredegar Ironworks, this was originally an Ebbw Vale Company pit, associated with their Sirhowy Ironworks nearby. (All Ebbw Vale collieries tended to be numbered, rather than named). In 1818, the Ebbw Vale Company was accused of being underhanded in the way it acquired the Tredegar-held Sirhowy-lease, an act which caused great hostility between the two Companies.

'Grahams' Navigation', so-named because it provided first-rate steam coal, was ventilated by means of a pit-bottom furnace. Hot gases rose up a brick-tube in the shaft, to be expelled via the tall chimney stack. Natural airflow over the chimney mouth created a partial vacuum which aided the process. Fresh air, replacing foul, flowed into the workings by way of another shaft higher up the mountainside. Until recent years it was possible to walk through old workings connecting Sirhowy and Ebbw Valleys.

A timber head-frame with double sheave stands over the shaft: Inside the hip-roofed engine house was a twin-cylinder steam winding engine. Beyond lay hundreds of acres of pit and ironworks waste, this having been the main waste disposal area for Sirhowy Works.

When the pit closed, its shaft, as was normal practice, was left open and unprotected. The buildings provided an easily-accessible adventure play-ground for local children, who would clamber around the shaft-mouth dropping stones into the water far below. Although it remained in this dangerous condition for perhaps fifty years, no one is recorded as having fallen-in. Several other open, and equally dangerous shafts were nearby.

GRAHAMS No 9 COLLIERY.   TREDEGAR   .2.

TRANSPORT - 'BOUGHT AND SOLD BY THE DOZEN'

Mule trains and their drivers figure in this 1790 illustration of coal being transported along the Taff Valley, from Merthyr to Cardiff.

Each animal carried three hundredweights (151 kgs.) on its back. A normal 'train' was of twelve mules or pack-horses transporting a total of 36 cwt. (1812 kgs.). Thus 'dozens' became a normal unit of trade. Mules were bred by crossing an ass with a mare and were a hardy animal. However, fodder was expensive and almost as many trains came back into the area carrying hay and corn as went out bearing coal and iron.

Two drivers, together with an odd number of mules, suggests that two 'dozens' were operating together. Different methods of loading the animals are indicated, well-balanced panniers contrasting with top-heavy sacks perched on pack-saddles. Even though pack-trains were replaced by tramroads, canals and steam locomotion, they lingered on: One was operating in the Brynmawr area until shortly before the 1939 War.

Taff Valley beauty, suggested by the drawing, was renowned and commented upon by contemporary tourists and others. The river was noted for its salmon, sometimes trapped in baskets fixed near water-falls; its cascades and woods being considered especially picturesque. During the hey-day of the coal industry, in common with all South Wales industrial valley-rivers, the Taff had become notorious for the coal-polluted blackness of its water.

TRANSPORT - 'PLATEWAYS'

A late Nineteenth Century photograph of a 'plateway' tramroad at Penderyn, near Hirwaun. Three horses, harnessed in tandem, move six trams each of which is loaded with several tons of limestone. Had this been on a normal road surface only a small part of this load would have been possible. Of interest is the manner in which the blocks are 'raced' (raised), common practice both above and below ground to get the maximum on each vehicle.

The L-shaped plates were designed so that their upright section kept tram-wheels on the flat base. Such wheels could be thinner and lighter, far less damaging, than those of a railroad system whereby wheels ran along rail-tops. So thin were these wheels that they were often referred to as 'knife-edged'.

In the foreground may be seen stone sleeper-blocks into which plates were pegged. Cast-iron 'tie-bars', holding plates a correct distance apart, are under a crushed limestone pathway for horses. Such plateways were common throughout the region, considered far more reliable, and less susceptible to breakage, than rail-roads. When descending steep gradients tram wheels were fixed into cast-iron shoes which caused them to skid, rather than revolve.

The high cost of purchasing and maintaining draught-animals, and the great numbers required, stimulated the development of steam locomotion. However, without the horse, mule and ass, the early development of industry would not have been possible in this remote upland region.

TRANSPORT - 'THE IRON HORSE'

A rare photograph of a saddle-tank locomotive working on an original plate-way. Taken some time after 1905 - the 'rebuild' date is shown on the cab - it has halted on the Trefil Tramroad during its journey to Tredegar Works. This industrial link had been designed for horse-traction one hundred years earlier; now this small engine and its one-man crew could move a load of limestone once requiring six or eight horses and their drivers. Even when maintenance and fuel costs were considered, steam locomotion was cheaper and more-efficient. That the locomotive was, in truth, an 'iron horse' is emphasized by the fact it pulls the original trams, some of which have wheel-camber indicating considerable age and wear.

This train, carrying Trefil limestone to Tredegar furnaces, had halted a short distance south of quarry and village. In the background is the line of another far more celebrated, but then-disused, tramroad namely Ben Hall's 'Brinore' of 1815 built to link his Rhymney Ironworks both with Trefil and, eight miles farther on, the canal at Talbont-on-Usk. It now provides one of the best scenic walks in Wales.

As was common practice the locomotive works cab-first on down gradients in order to retain a correct boiler-water level over the fire-box. It also lessened the ever-present danger of unbraked trams and wagons becoming runaways - these being a frequent occurrence sometimes causing fatalities.

A large steam-whistle mounted on its cab roof was essential equipment; this train would cross busy streets during its journey.

EARLY PIT-WORKERS

Specialised industrial clothing did not exist; men and women wore normal everyday garb of the period. This drawing, made in the early part of the century shows Merthyr Tydfil workers against a background of the furnaces they toiled to supply.

Two women have blackened faces indicating possibly that their work was underground: Others are cleaner but all have their heads covered by scarves. Hats became a tradition, most women surface-workers eventually wearing feathered headgear, no matter how dirty the employment. The male colliers wear low, flat-brimmed, hats in which are stuck the candles needed to light their working-place; sometimes these would be fixed to the brim with a ball of clay. A hand oil-lamp is carried, both to give light, and re-ignite candles. Cloth bags slung over shoulders possibly contained food and water as well as other essentials; these would be hung in places rats might not reach. Trousers are tucked into boot-tops, making kneeling easier and preventing rats entering.

Metal food and water containers are shown. These essential vermin-proof, vessels were usually of local manufacture, tin-smithing being an important occupation in most mining-towns. Even chewing or smoking tobacco would be kept in small, air-tight, tin or brass boxes.

TREDEGAR MINER (Mid-Nineteenth Century)

Typically wearing what had once been everyday clothing, this young man must have been photographed shortly after completing an underground shift. The Tredegar photographer made a collection of such studies and so created a fascinating social record.

The jacket was made for a larger person - 'handing-down' clothes was a normal practice in all working areas, nothing being thrown away until completely worn out. Similarly, his hat might be one that was re-used and cut-down. Over his shoulder is slung a food-bag; in one hand is the essential water-jack, whilst in the other is a 'ball and peg' oil lamp. These naked-flame lights were provided with a spike enabling them to be stuck into timber prop or working face. Around his neck is a scarf, better-known in this region as a 'muffler', worn to keep out dust and grit: The muffler became an essential element of both work and leisure wear throughout industrial South Wales. Until recent times the off-duty collier's uniform was navy-blue suit, white muffler, and cloth ('Dai') cap.

Although tiredness after a long shift is apparent, the dirt does not seem to be that of coal dust and might indicate that he worked extracting iron-stone or 'mine'. If this was, indeed, the case, he would have been a 'miner' rather than a 'coal-ier', i.e. 'collier'.

Well-nourished, he possesses the developed upper body and arms of the manual worker. In contrast his legs seem thin, a normal attribute of those who spent long hours crouching or lying in restricted spaces.

Should he survive sickness and accident this miner would have been forced to go on working as long as he was able. There was no pension to provide for old age.

TREDEGAR PIT-GIRL, c. 1860

Looking older than her probable fourteen years, this Tredegar pit-girl was one of several recorded by a local photographer before the same painted back-cloth. She wears what appears to be a button-decorated skull-cap, or cut-down hat, over a knotted head-scarf. Possibly her work was in low-roofed places, and may have entailed moving trams.

A dress, once of good quality, has been shortened but, even so, is caked with mud and torn. A tin food-box and water-jack plus heavy boots with wollen stockings make up her working attire. Interestingly, she seems sturdy and well-nourished.

By this time in the century she may well have been born in the town to parents who had arrived earlier. However, there are several recorded instances of young girls running away from countryside homes to seek work and prosperity in the iron towns. Apart from the real physical dangers of such employment, presentable females always risked seduction by unscrupulous overseers and managers. Marriage was the only solution; unless there were exceptional circumstances married woman did not go to work.

TREDEGAR PIT-BOY, c. 1860

Wearing a cap padded with rags or paper, a common practice until safety-helmets were introduced, this young pit-worker has a candle tucked into its brim. Two pairs of trousers, one worn over the other and stained with water and mud, give some indication of the conditions in which he worked.

A safety lamp is carried suggesting that his working place would be tested for gas before the candle was lit: Certainly in latter days this would have been the task of an overman or 'firemen' who would test all workings before men entered. 'Davy' safety-lamps were unpopular with early underground workers because they provided less light than candles: Another reason for this dislike was that dangerously-gaseous districts could now be worked. Apart from explosive gases there was the heavier-than-air 'Black Damp' which could suffocate quickly.

In primitive conditions, where roadways and workings were supported by timber props, the roof might collapse at any time. Coal seams could emit explosive or suffocating gases making what had previously been safe for naked lights to explode in a ball of flames. In early pits a moment's carelessness could cause injury or death. Until quite recent times serious pit accidents were, sadly, commonplace.

DOG-FIGHTING, MERTHYR TYDFIL, C. 1880

('Illustrated London News')

Similar scenes might have been witnessed in any iron-town of the period. Variously-clad men - one is barefoot - watch dogs being matched against each other. Another animal is held, perhaps to challenge the eventual winner? Bets are being placed and a spectator signals to a book-maker whose clerk sits at a table. There is a bucket, possibly filled with water to revive dogs, or with sawdust to soak up blood. It is noticeable that no women are present.

Other popular sporting activities were bare-fist fighting and foot-racing, with much money being wagered. Such events provided opportunities for local stars to test themselves against professionals, a tradition lingering on in the boxing-booths of later fairs. One local fight was of special significance although there were few witnesses and no bets were laid. On a Sunday night in 1840 Shoni Ysgubor Fawr, i.e. 'Johhny Of Big Barn', who was Champion Prize-fighter of All Wales, also 'Emperor Of China', (China being a local nest of villainy), was soundly thrashed in fair fight by Police Sgt. Evan Davies. Above all else it indicated that the recently-established force was one to be reckoned with.

The tradition of open-air gambling became deep-rooted throughout the region and was to continue until legalization. Notorious were the gambling 'schools' gathered every Sunday on remoter tips or areas of waste ground, look-outs being posted to warn of police approach.

HOUSES AND INDUSTRY - VICTORIA, EBBW VALE

Dating from the latter part of the Nineteenth Century, this photograph makes clear how closely housing and industry were then related. Here, Ebbw Vale works stacks and pit-shafts almost intermingle with houses; in the days before cheap public transport it was normal for workers to live as near to their place of employment as possible. At Blaenavon Iron-works, for example, such proximity was even greater, 'Stack Square' workers' housing, alongside the furnaces, was so-named because of a large industrial boiler-stack at its centre.

The area shown lay just north of where, in 1992, Garden Festival - Wales was to be sited. Long rows of houses, two-storeyed in front, three at their rear where the ground sloped away, overlook a narrow access lane and surprisingly large gardens. Coal-cots, pigsties and ty-bachs, ('little houses', i.e. privies), stood here, night-soil from then being carted away to be dumped. Not all homes possessed such good sanitary arrangements; some privies were no more than holes dug into the earth.

A saddle-tank, open-cab, locomotive working cab-first down the gradient, waits to collect a train of small heavy-duty wagons. It was a Monday, washing-day; a pall of industrial fume moves down over clean articles pegged out to dry.

Perhaps significantly in days when accidents were frequent the seated figure in the fore-ground appears crippled, a pair of crutches lie near him on the ground.

COLLIERS AND BUTTIES - POCHIN PIT, TREDEGAR

A surprising number of young boys, colliers' 'butties' or trainees, usually sons or relatives learning the craft, make this c. 1910 photograph remarkable. Since every worker was entitled to be kept supplied with a tram, this doubled the possible output and pay. Cloth or paper-padded caps, Davy lamps, tin food-boxes and water-jacks are typical. Still being worn are tightly-wrapped neck-cloths or 'mufflers' to exclude dust and grit. One boy wears 'yorks', i.e. leather straps ties beneath the knees. In mining folk-lore these were 'to keep the rats from running up trousers' and there were, certainly, great numbers of these creatures in almost every pit. A more mudane reason was that yorks bagged-out the trouser-legs making it easier and more comfortable to kneel.

These pit workers had gone down the shaft early that morning - many experienced colliers would arrive at the coal-face before time so that they could make everything safe. All might have walked long distances from pit-bottom in those days before underground transport, to spend every possible minute timbering, cutting coal and filling trams. There were no 'toilets', other than the dangerous gobs, voids from which coal had been extracted. Human faeces, pony-fodder and discarded food scraps maintained the rat swarms.

Pit head baths did not become usual for many years and every collier's household would possess a 'tin' tub which, filled with hot water, would be placed before the kitchen fire. When a colliers' train arrived, town streets would fill with hundreds of tired and dirty men as they trudged home to a waiting bath and meal.

POCHIN COLLIERS JUST OUT OF THE PIT. WAITING FOR THE 3 50 TRAIN. 340

TREDEGAR SHOP c. 1900

This shop on Georgetown Hill, Tredegar, is still in use as a Post Office and Stores. It was typical of its period, the goods on sale telling much about the life-style of its customers.

Other than the window display of canned goods, usually considered too expensive, or dismissed as inferior, such a shop would sell most everyday requirements from bulk sack, cask, or boxes. Sugar, tea, treacle, butter, bacon, biscuits, vinegar, would be individually weighed and packed. Butter, especially, required great skill to serve, cut from huge blocks to be shaped between wooden 'pats' and then stamped with an engraved block. Apart from food-stuffs such items as candles, paraffin and firewood would be available, indeed almost everything necessary for the average collier's or steel-worker's household.

Outside, on the pavement, are potatoes and other vegetables whilst white-washing brushes, essential for interior and exterior decoration, hang over the door.

Clearly indicated is the importance of washing, clothes or person, in this town of heavy industry. Here are the 'tin-tubs' serving equally for laundry and bathing; alongside are the galvanised pails with which they would be filled from a fire-side boiler. 'Dollies' for agitating the wash hung not far from corrugated scrubbing-boards on which especially dirty items would be rubbed. Soap of various kinds, together with the 'blue' to make whites look whiter, are available. Monday, i.e. Washing Day, was especially hard for women with large families, not least because every wife would be judged by the appearance of what she hung out to dry.

These were days of surprisingly high standards; even the two shop-men wear white jackets and aprons, together with very formal collars and ties.

'GOING HOME'

On a damp Tredegar afternoon in 1956, photographer Gordon Hayward recorded these two colliers walking home from 'Ty Trist' pit, across the valley. Taking its name from the goblin-haunted 'House Of Sorrow' farm on whose lands it had been sunk, the pit stood in an area of industrial waste, partly of its own creation, partly that of another pit nearby. Other than 'Mill Farm', an ancient farm-site in the foreground, the whole valley floor was covered by iron-slag. The River Sirhowy flows through a man-made ravine; this southern part of Tredegar even today being referred to as 'down the tip'. Pock-marks left by 'patching' - in this case from times of strike when men scraped for fuel - can be seen, and yet enough original landscape remains for the region to be classified as 'semi-rural'.

An underground worker's life had changed little in the past one hundred years. He might still live close to his pit and walk to and from work both above and below ground; by this time Ty Trist worked seams far from pit-bottom. Both men have their trousers tied up with 'yorks' and wear cloth caps similar to those their fore-bears wore long before. However, no women and children now worked underground and open-flame lights had given way to electric safety lamps, unpopular because of their weight: Steel-toed boots were now essential. Main roadways were supported by steel 'Tredegar-rings', invented in the town and used throughout the world. Both men are black with coal dust but, at this period, they might wash it off in a bathroom, although for some there were still tubs in front of the fire.

No one knew then that their pit, together with all others in the area were doomed. Ty Trist would close three years later, worked-out after nearly a century of production. By 1992, year of Garden Festival - Wales, only three Welsh pits survive, fewer than could be seen in 1956 from where this photograph was taken.